THE INDIAN EPICS RETOLD

A CONTEMPORARY INTERPRETATION OF THE RAMAYANA AND THE MAHABHARATA

DR. JAGADEESH PILLAI

Copyright © Dr. Jagadeesh Pillai
All Rights Reserved.

This book has been self-published with all reasonable efforts taken to make the material error-free by the author. No part of this book shall be used, reproduced in any manner whatsoever without written permission from the author, except in the case of brief quotations embodied in critical articles and reviews.

The Author of this book is solely responsible and liable for its content including but not limited to the views, representations, descriptions, statements, information, opinions and references ["Content"]. The Content of this book shall not constitute or be construed or deemed to reflect the opinion or expression of the Publisher or Editor. Neither the Publisher nor Editor endorse or approve the Content of this book or guarantee the reliability, accuracy or completeness of the Content published herein and do not make any representations or warranties of any kind, express or implied, including but not limited to the implied warranties of merchantability, fitness for a particular purpose. The Publisher and Editor shall not be liable whatsoever for any errors, omissions, whether such errors or omissions result from negligence, accident, or any other cause or claims for loss or damages of any kind, including without limitation, indirect or consequential loss or damage arising out of use, inability to use, or about the reliability, accuracy or sufficiency of the information contained in this book.

Made with ♥ on the Notion Press Platform
www.notionpress.com

|| "Dedicated to all who seek to understand and appreciate Indian culture and tradition." ||

Contents

Contents

Prayer

"Om Sahanaa Vavatu Sahanau BhunaktuSaha Veeryam KaravaavahaiTejasvi Naavadheetamastu Maa VidvishaavahaiOm Shantih Shantih Shantih"

The literal interpretation of this mantra is: OM. Let us all protect one another, let us all share in joy, let us all work together and let our learning be illuminated. Let us be united in peace,
OM Peace, Peace, Peace.

❦❦❦

About The Author

Dr. Jagadeesh Pillai is a renowned Guinness World Record holder, writer, and researcher hailing from Varanasi, also known as the abode of Lord Shiva. With a Ph.D. in Vedic Science and a range of creative ideas and achievements, he is a true polymath. He is the author of more than 100 books including Research Publications. Although his roots can be traced back to Kerala, the people of Varanasi hold him in high regard and affectionately consider him one of their own.

Dr. Pillai has achieved four Guinness World Records in the following subjects:

"Script to Screen" - In this record, Dr. Pillai produced and directed an animation film within the shortest time possible, breaking the previous record set by Canadians. He has also received numerous national and international awards and recognitions for this achievement.

Longest Line of Postcards - For this record, Dr. Pillai created a line of 16,300 postcards on the occasion of the 163rd anniversary of Indian Postal Day. The event also included a questionnaire about the Indian flag.

Largest Poster Awareness Campaign - Dr. Pillai designed an awareness campaign on the subject of "Beti Bachao - Beti Padhao" (Save the Girl Child - Educate the Girl Child) to achieve this record.

Largest Envelope - In tribute to the Indian Prime Minister's

"Make in India" initiative, Dr. Pillai created a 4000 square meter envelope using waste paper to achieve this record.

Attempted - **70000 Candles on a 210 kg Cake** - To celebrate the 70th Indian Independence Day, Dr. Pillai attempted to light 70,000 candles on a 210 kg cake, which was recorded in World Records India.

Attempted - **Documentary on Dhamek Stupa of Sarnath in 17 Languages** - Dr. Pillai attempted to create a documentary on the Dhamek Stupa of Sarnath, dubbing it in 17 different languages. The result of this attempt is currently awaiting confirmation from the Guinness World Records.

Dr. Pillai is skilled in teaching the Bhagavad Gita, a Hindu scripture, and is popular among young people. He has helped many young people improve their lives through his motivational teachings.

In addition to teaching, he has composed and sung numerous Sanskrit Bhajans and patriotic songs.

He has also written and directed several short films and documentaries for awareness campaigns, and has volunteered with the police in both UP and Kerala to spread awareness about various issues through videos and photography.

Incredibly, he has produced and directed over 100 documentaries about the city of Varanasi, all on his own.

He has also helped and guided more than 25 boys and girls to achieve world records through creative and innovative methods. He is a multifaceted person who uses his intellect and the blessings given to him by God to excel in various areas. He is both a teacher and a student, always learning and teaching, and is able to master any subject he comes across.

He is a selfless social activist and motivational speaker who has overcome struggles and failures to become a successful and enthusiastic individual with a rich life experience.

In addition to his work with the Bhagavad Gita, he is also an efficient Tarot card reader, Astro-Vastu consultant, and a talented singer and composer. He has sung the entire Ram Charita Manas and Bhagavad Gita in his own compositions, and has sung the phrase "Lokah Samastha Sukhino Bhavantu" in 50 different languages. He is currently working on a detailed and scientific study of Vedas, Upanishads, Puranas, and the Bhagavad Gita. He has also composed and sung the Hanuman Chalisa and Gayatri Mantra in 108 and 1008 different compositions, respectively.

Awards - Four Times Guinness World Records, Winner of Mahatma Gandhi Vishwa Shanti Puraskar, Mahatma Gandhi Global Peace Ambassador, Kashi Ratna Award, Dr. APJ Abdul Kalam Motivational Person of the Year 2017, Mother Teresa Award, Indira Gandhi Priyadarshini Award, Bharat Vikas Ratna Award, Udyog Ratna Award, Vigyan Prasar Award, Poorvanchal Ratn Samman.

ᏇᏇᏇ

Preface

The Ramayana and Mahabharata are two of the most important and enduring texts in Indian culture, with stories and characters that have shaped the cultural and moral values of the Indian people for centuries. These epics have been passed down through generations and continue to be an integral part of Indian society today.

This book, "The Indian Epics Retold: A Contemporary Interpretation of the Ramayana and the Mahabharata," aims to explore these ancient texts in a modern context. It provides an in-depth analysis of the stories and characters, and examines the themes and motifs that continue to resonate with readers today.

The book also delves into the influence of the Ramayana and Mahabharata on Southeast Asian culture and how these epics have shaped the cultural heritage of the region. It also examines the adaptations and retellings of these epics in modern literature, film and other forms of art, and how they have been adapted to address contemporary issues and concerns.

The book is intended for readers who are interested in gaining a deeper understanding of these ancient texts and their relevance to contemporary society. It is written for both the general reader and the academic, and provides a fresh and nuanced perspective on these ancient epics.

With this book, we hope to provide a deeper understanding of the Ramayana and Mahabharata and their continued relevance to the modern world.

ᛞᛞᛞ

ONE

SIGNIFICANCE OF RAMAYANA AND MAHABHARATA

The Ramayana and the Mahabharata are two of the most revered and significant texts in Indian culture. These epics, which were written in Sanskrit, have been passed down through generations and continue to be widely read and studied today. They are not just stories, but also serve as a guide for moral conduct, a source of inspiration, and a reflection of Indian culture and values.

The Ramayana, written by Sage Valmiki, is the story of Prince Rama, who is considered an incarnation of the Hindu god Vishnu. The epic tells the story of Rama's journey to rescue his wife Sita, who has been kidnapped by the demon king, Ravana. The story is filled with adventures and battles, but also deals with themes of love, duty, and the importance of following dharma (moral and ethical code).

The Mahabharata, written by Sage Vyasa, is a much longer epic that tells the story of a war between the Pandavas and the Kauravas, two branches of the same family. The story is not just about the war, but also deals with themes such as the nature of right and wrong, the meaning of righteousness, and the importance of family. The epic also includes the Bhagavad Gita, a text that is considered one of the most important works in Hindu philosophy.

Both the Ramayana and the Mahabharata have had a profound influence on Indian culture and continue to be widely read and studied today. They are not just stories, but also serve as a guide for moral conduct, a source of inspiration, and a reflection of Indian culture and values.

In this book, we will explore the Ramayana and the Mahabharata in a new light, examining their themes and characters through a contemporary lens. We will also look at how these ancient texts continue to be relevant today, and how they have been retold and adapted in different forms of media such as film, television, and comics. Our aim is to provide a fresh and accessible interpretation of these timeless epics, and to encourage readers to explore these stories in a deeper and more meaningful way.

ppp

"The mind is everything; what you think, you become." - Bhagavad Gita

TWO

THE RAMAYANA: AN OVERVIEW

The Ramayana, written by Sage Valmiki, is one of the two major Sanskrit epics of ancient India, the other being the Mahabharata. It tells the story of Prince Rama, who is considered an incarnation of the Hindu god Vishnu. The epic is divided into seven books, known as kandas, and follows Rama's journey to rescue his wife Sita, who has been kidnapped by the demon king, Ravana.

The story begins with the introduction of Rama, the prince of Ayodhya, who is the eldest son of King Dasharatha. Rama is loved and respected by all, and is seen as the ideal prince and future king. However, his stepmother, Kaikeyi, demands that her own son, Bharata, be made king instead. Rama, being a dutiful son, agrees to go into exile for 14 years, along with his wife Sita and brother Lakshmana.

During their exile, Sita is kidnapped by Ravana, the demon king of Lanka. Rama, with the help of an army of monkeys and bears, led by the monkey king Hanuman, launches a campaign to rescue Sita. After many battles and adventures, Rama and his army ultimately defeat Ravana and rescue Sita.

The epic also deals with themes such as the importance of duty and loyalty, the power of devotion and faith, and the ultimate triumph of good over evil. The story of Rama is not just a story of adventure and war, but also serves as a guide for moral conduct and a reflection of Indian culture and values.

The Ramayana has had a profound influence on Indian culture and continues to be widely read and studied today. It is also widely popular in Southeast Asia, particularly in Indonesia, where it is known as the Ramakien. The Ramayana has been retold and adapted in different forms of media such as film, television, and comics, making it accessible to a wide audience.

᭢᭢᭢

"One who is steadfast in yoga, who fully engages the mind and the senses in the pursuit of the ultimate goal, attains the supreme goal of life." - Bhagavad Gita

THREE

RAMA: THE IDEAL KING

Rama, the protagonist of the Ramayana, is considered the ideal king and an embodiment of dharma (moral and ethical code) in Indian culture. He is known for his courage, wisdom, and compassion, and is admired for his devotion to duty and loyalty to his family and subjects.

Rama's story begins with his childhood as the eldest son of King Dasharatha of Ayodhya. From a young age, he is known for his bravery, wisdom, and good character. He is loved and respected by all, and is seen as the ideal prince and future king. However, his stepmother, Kaikeyi, demands that her own son, Bharata, be made king instead. Rama, being a dutiful son, agrees to go into exile for 14 years, along with his wife Sita and brother Lakshmana.

During his exile, Rama demonstrates his courage and wisdom in many ways. He battles demons and monsters, and always acts with compassion and fairness. He also remains steadfast in his devotion to Sita, even when she is kidnapped by the demon king, Ravana. He leads an army of monkeys and bears to rescue her, and ultimately defeats Ravana and rescues Sita.

One of the key themes of the Ramayana is the importance of duty and loyalty. Rama is a symbol of this, as he always puts his duty to his family and subjects before his own desires. He also demonstrates the importance of being true to one's word, as he keeps his promise to go into exile, even though it causes him great personal pain.

Rama's character is also an embodiment of the Hindu concept of "Rajdharma", which means the code of conduct for a king. It is believed that a king should be an exemplar of virtues such as justice, fortitude, and compassion. Rama is seen as the perfect example of this, as he always acts with fairness and compassion, and puts the well-being of his subjects before his own desires.

Rama, the protagonist of the Ramayana, is considered the ideal king and an embodiment of dharma, duty and loyalty. He is admired for his devotion to duty, wisdom, courage, compassion, and his adherence to Rajdharma in Indian culture and mythology.

ᐅᐅᐅ

"The world is sustained by three things: truth, righteousness, and compassion." - Mahabharata

FOUR
SITA: THE IDEAL CONSORT

The epic poem Ramayana is an iconic tale unfolding the story of Rama, an incarnation of Vishnu the protector of the Universe, and his perfect relationship and companionship with his wife Sita. The reason for Rama and Sita's presence in mythology is not merely to showcase a holy marital bond, or to illustrate the power of divine love, but to depict a perfect model of the Indian ideal wife.

Sita, an incarnation of goddess Lakshmi, is the perfect consort to her husband and the ideal woman in Hindu mythology. She is born from the earth as a fully mature woman compelling all the gods to bow before her beauty and brilliance. From the very first day that Sita steps into Ram's life, her beauty and strength add colors, life, and hope. She allures him with her ideal, traditional virtues and is characteristically just, kind, humble and honest.

Not only is Sita a loyal and devoted wife but she is also cognitively wise. Throughout her lifetime Sita is determined and devoted to keep her husband's honour intact. When Rama realizes that Sita's reputation is in danger because of the challenges to her purity, Sita willingly goes into exile driven by her sense of religious piety and devotion to Rama. Self-sacrifice is indeed one of Sita's biggest virtues and she even proves her dedication and pure heart by undergoing Agni pariksha (test of purity by fire).

Sita is also a symbol of feminine strength and fortitude and her unwavering devotion to Rama even in challenging times like her exile demonstrate her strength of character. She stands firm with Rama and inspires even Rama to stay strong in trying times.

Sita is indeed the perfect consort to Rama as she is able to challenge him to stay noble and often remind him of his duty and dharma as an ideal king. She helps him throughout his journey and it is her self-sacrificing personality and unparalleled devotion that make this couple the ideal couple of Ramayana and an iconic symbol of marital bliss.

ԷԷԷ

"The one who is steadfast in devotion, who is free from attachment, who is free from enmity, who is free from pride and is always content, such a person attains the supreme goal." - Bhagavad Gita

FIVE
THE MAHABHARATA: AN OVERVIEW

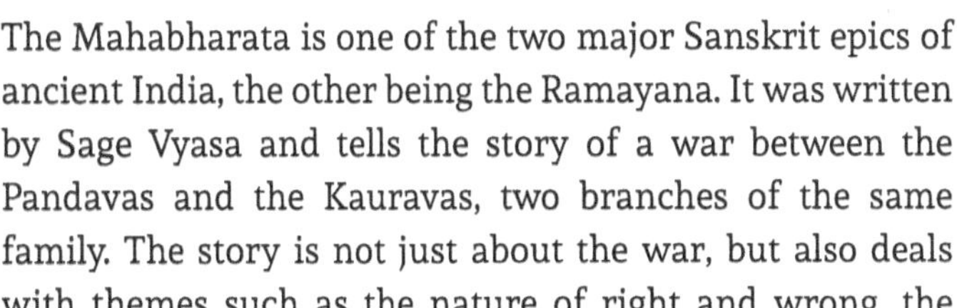

The Mahabharata is one of the two major Sanskrit epics of ancient India, the other being the Ramayana. It was written by Sage Vyasa and tells the story of a war between the Pandavas and the Kauravas, two branches of the same family. The story is not just about the war, but also deals with themes such as the nature of right and wrong, the meaning of righteousness, and the importance of family.

The Mahabharata begins with the story of King Shantanu and his son, Bhishma. Bhishma is a powerful warrior and is known for his devotion to his father and his adherence to dharma (moral and ethical code). However, as he grows older, he becomes increasingly aware of the weaknesses and flaws of the Kuru dynasty, of which he is a member.

The story then shifts to the Pandavas, five brothers, and

their cousin, Duryodhana, who is the eldest of the Kauravas. The Pandavas and the Kauravas have a long-standing feud, and the story progresses with their conflicts and battles, ultimately leading to a great war. The Pandavas, who are the rightful heirs to the kingdom, are forced to fight for their kingdom and their rights against the Kauravas, who refuse to give up their claim to the throne.

The war lasts for 18 days and results in the deaths of many great warriors on both sides. The Pandavas ultimately emerge victorious, but the war leaves the kingdom in ruins and the victors with heavy hearts.

The Mahabharata also includes the Bhagavad Gita, a text that is considered one of the most important works in Hindu philosophy. It is a dialogue between Lord Krishna, who serves as a guide and mentor to the Pandava prince Arjuna, and Arjuna, who is in a moral dilemma about fighting his own kin in the war. The Bhagavad Gita is considered a masterpiece of spiritual and ethical teachings, and is widely studied and revered in Hinduism.

The Mahabharata is not just a story of war, but also deals with themes such as the nature of right and wrong, the meaning of righteousness, and the importance of family. It is a complex and multi-layered epic that explores the human condition, and raises fundamental questions about the nature of existence, the purpose of life and the ultimate destiny of man. The epic also includes the Bhagavad Gita, one of the most important works in Hindu philosophy, which is widely studied and revered in Hinduism.

ᐳᐳᐳ

"The one who sees the unity of all living beings in their diversity and diversity in their unity, attains the highest level of spiritual understanding." - Bhagavad Gita

SIX

THE RAMAYANA AND MAHABHARATA IN THE MODERN WORLD.

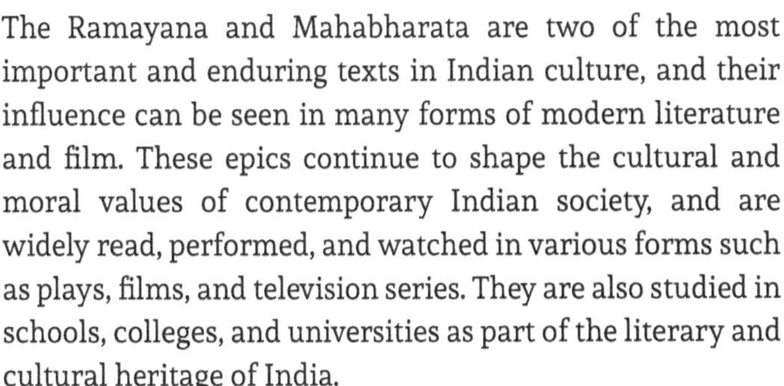

The Ramayana and Mahabharata are two of the most important and enduring texts in Indian culture, and their influence can be seen in many forms of modern literature and film. These epics continue to shape the cultural and moral values of contemporary Indian society, and are widely read, performed, and watched in various forms such as plays, films, and television series. They are also studied in schools, colleges, and universities as part of the literary and cultural heritage of India.

Additionally, these epics have had a significant impact on

Southeast Asian culture, and continue to be an important part of the cultural heritage of many countries in the region. They are widely performed and watched, taught in schools as part of the national curriculum and considered a fundamental part of the culture.

The stories and characters of the Ramayana and Mahabharata are deeply ingrained in the collective consciousness of the Indian people and Southeast Asian people, and they continue to provide a cultural context for many of the customs and traditions of India and Southeast Asia.

The themes of the epics have also been adapted to address contemporary issues and concerns, such as the promotion of gender equality and non-violence. They are not only a source of entertainment but also a source of inspiration and guidance for people in the modern world.

The Ramayana and Mahabharata are two of the most important and enduring texts in Indian culture and Southeast Asian culture, and continue to shape the cultural and moral values of contemporary society through various forms of literature, film and performance. They are not only a source of entertainment but also a source of inspiration and guidance for people in the modern world.

ॐॐॐ

"One who is able to endure hardship, who is not agitated by suffering, who is steady in happiness and sorrow, such a person is dear to me." - Bhagavad Gita

SEVEN

THE PANDAVAS: THE HEROES OF THE MAHABHARATA

The Mahabharata is one of the great Hindu epics and is filled with a variety of characters, both heroic and villainous. Among them are the Pandavas, a group of five brothers, who are some of the most beloved and celebrated heroes in the epic. Each of the five brothers has their own distinct personality and contributions, making them an inspiring and legendary group.

The eldest of the Pandavas is Yudhishthira, who epitomizes righteousness. Known as 'Dharma-raja', Yudhishthira is noble, wise, and fair-minded, embodying the ideals of Dharma. He is the king of the Pandavas and leads them through the Mahabharata war, relying on his moral judgement to make difficult decisions. He is skilled in philosophical debates and wise counsel, and despite his temptations and sufferings, Yudhishthira remains faithful to Dharma.

The second eldest, Bhima, is renowned for his immense strength and bravery in battle. He is a powerful warrior, capable of taking on multiple adversaries and fighting even the gods themselves. He is an emotionally volatile man, and this anger often propels him to great acts of heroism, especially during the Mahabharata war. Bhima is also renowned for his kind heart and sense of justice, using his strength to protect those in need.

The third Pandava is Arjuna, the ultimate archer and champion of the Mahabharata war. He is known for his great skill with the bow, capable of shooting arrows with pinpoint accuracy. He is a formidable opponent in battle, and alone is more powerful than an army. He is also an exceptional fighter, often facing seemingly impossible odds and coming out victorious. Arjuna also has a compassionate heart and is known for his love and devotion to Lord Krishna and his family.

The fourth brother is Nakula, who is known for his extraordinary beauty and expertise in warfare. He is one of the most skilled martial artists in the Mahabharata and his abilities are revered by the gods. He is also an accomplished horseman, often taking the lead in battle and manoeuvring with extreme agility and speed. He is also a great fighter, known for his cool, calculating skills and peerless swordplay.

The youngest Pandava is Sahadeva, who epitomizes

wisdom and intelligence. He is a skilled scholar, known for his vast knowledge of scriptures, languages, and the arts. Sahadeva is also renowned for his prophetic powers and the ability to foretell the future. He is an invaluable asset to the Pandavas during the Mahabharata war and his counsel gains them many victories.

The Pandavas stand as exemplars of courage and righteousness, with each brother having their own unique capabilities and contributions to the Mahabharata. From Yudhishthira's leadership and strategy, to Bhima's physical strength and courage, to Nakula and Sahadeva's expertise in various arts, they all played a vital role in the great battle of Kurukshetra. Together, they stood against the Kauravas, who represented deceit and unrighteousness, and emerged victorious. The Pandavas' story teaches us valuable lessons about the importance of righteousness, courage, and the power of unity in the face of adversity."

ᘒᘒᘒ

"The one who controls their mind, they control their life. The one who controls their breath, they control their mind." - Bhagavad Gita

EIGHT

THE KAURAVAS: THE VILLAINS OF THE MAHABHARATA

In the Mahabharata, the Kauravas are portrayed as the main antagonists of the story, who are in conflict with the Pandavas, the five brothers who are the rightful heirs to the kingdom. The Kauravas, led by Duryodhana, are the eldest sons of King Dhritarashtra and are determined to keep the kingdom for themselves, even though the Pandavas have the legal claim to it.

Throughout the epic, the Kauravas are portrayed as ruthless and power-hungry, willing to do whatever it takes to maintain their hold on the kingdom. They cheat and deceive in order to defeat the Pandavas in various contests, and even go so far as to try to kill them by setting their palace on fire. They also refuse to give up their claim to the kingdom, even when it becomes clear that the Pandavas are the rightful heirs.

The Kauravas are also depicted as lacking in moral and ethical principles, and are motivated solely by their desire for power and wealth. They are portrayed as being consumed by envy and hatred towards the Pandavas, and are willing to do anything to defeat them, even if it means resorting to underhanded tactics and breaking the rules of war.

Despite their negative portrayal in the epic, the Kauravas are also complex characters, and their actions are not always entirely unjustified. They are also seen as victims of fate and circumstance, as they are born into a family where power is in question and the kingdom is split between two branches of the same family.

In the Mahabharata, the Kauravas are portrayed as the main antagonists of the story, who are in conflict with the Pandavas, the five brothers who are the rightful heirs to the kingdom. They are portrayed as ruthless, power-hungry and lacking in moral and ethical principles, willing to do whatever it takes to maintain their hold on the kingdom, even if it means resorting to underhanded tactics and breaking the rules of war. However, they are also complex characters, and their actions are not always entirely unjustified.

ᐅᐅᐅ

"The one who sees inaction in action, and action in inaction, they are wise among mortals. They have achieved the ultimate goal." - Bhagavad Gita

NINE

THE ROLE OF THE DIVINE IN THE RAMAYANA AND MAHABHARATA

The Ramayana and Mahabharata are both set in a world where the divine and the mortal coexist and interact with each other. The gods and goddesses, as well as other divine beings, play a significant role in the stories, both as characters and as forces that shape the events of the epic.

In the Ramayana, the gods play a more direct role in the story. Rama, the protagonist, is an incarnation of the god Vishnu, and his actions are guided by the gods throughout the story. The gods also directly intervene in the story, such as when they provide Rama with the powerful weapon, the "Brahmastra" to defeat the demon king, Ravana.

In the Mahabharata, the gods play a more subtle role, but

are still present throughout the story. They are often invoked by the characters in times of need, and their blessings and curses shape the events of the epic. The gods also appear in disguise and interact with the characters, such as when Lord Krishna, an incarnation of Vishnu, serves as a guide and mentor to the Pandava prince Arjuna.

Both epics also deal with the theme of fate, and how the actions of the gods and other divine forces shape the lives of the characters. The characters often seek the blessings of the gods and try to understand the will of the gods in order to navigate the events of the epic.

Additionally, the epics also explore the idea of karma, the belief that one's actions in this life determine one's fate in the next. The characters in the epics are often seen to be reaping the consequences of their past actions, and the gods are seen as dispensing justice according to the laws of karma.

The Ramayana and Mahabharata are both set in a world where the divine and the mortal coexist and interact with each other. The gods and goddesses, as well as other divine beings, play a significant role in the stories, both as characters and as forces that shape the events of the epic. Both epics also deal with the theme of fate and karma, the belief that one's actions in this life determine one's fate in the next, and how the actions of the gods and other divine forces shape the lives of the characters.

ᎮᎮᎮ

*"Be steadfast in yoga, O Arjuna. Perform your duty and abandon all attachment to success or failure. Such evenness of mind is called yoga." -
Bhagavad Gita*

TEN

THE CONCEPT OF DHARMA IN THE EPICS

Deeply embedded within the culturally rich heritage of Indian scriptures is the concept of the Dharma. Dharma is defined broadly as the moral law that governs all life and is considered the spritiual foundation of society. It is an integral part of Hindu philosophy and is believed to uphold the harmony and balance of the universe. The great Indian epics Ramayana and Mahabharata serve as important sources for understanding the concept of Dharma, particularly in terms of its relevance to practical life.

The Ramayana is essentially a tale of virtue and piety. The characters of the Ramayana are but mirrors of the virtues of dharma that are instilled in us. The epic follows the story of Rama and his wife Sita, the protagonists, in their struggle against the demon king Ravana. Imbued in the Ramayana is the notion that any action should always pass the test of justice and fairness. Rama was an ideal representation of Dharma as his life exemplified selfless devotion; despite immense adversity, he never resorted to revenge and aggression. He continually reminded himself, and those around him, of his dharma, urging them to seek the path of righteousness.

The Mahabharata is a complex narrative of spiritual dharma. It tells the tale of the ancient royal family of the Kuru dynasty, the Pandavas, and their quest to seek justice against their cousins, the Kauravas. With its theme of "Dharma Yudha" (righteous war), the epic outlines of the concept of dharma by elaborating on the underlying principles of conflict resolution. Those who follow the path of dharma will be rewarded, while those who deviate from it face harsh consequences. In the Mahabharata, these Dharmic principles are exemplified by Yudhisthira's adherence to the truth and his refusal to take the path of revenge, irrespective of the hurdles he faced.

The epics of Ramayana and Mahabharata are heavy with lessons on dharma and morality. They offer unique insight into the concept of dharma and its relevance in everyday life. Through the examples of Rama and Yudhisthira, and their adherence to the moral law of dharma, the epics demonstrate the positive outcomes that result from living in harmony with oneself and others. The epics of Ramayana and Mahabharata serve as a reminder of the ideal way of life and illustrate the benefits of living in accordance with the path of righteousness and justice.

ᐱᐱᐱ

"Like the butter hidden in milk, pure consciousness resides within every being, waiting to be revealed through the churning power of the mind. This inner wisdom can be unlocked through contemplation and introspection, allowing us to uncover the hidden depths of our being and discover our true potential." - Amrita-Bindu Upanishad

ELEVEN

THE RAMAYANA AND MAHABHARATA IN MODERN LITERATURE AND FILM

The Ramayana and Mahabharata are two of the most important and enduring texts in Indian culture, and their influence can be seen in many forms of modern literature and film.

In literature, both epics have been retold and reinterpreted in various forms, such as novels, poetry, and plays. Many contemporary Indian authors have written novels, short stories and poetry inspired by the epics, often bringing new perspectives and themes to the classic stories.

In film and television, the Ramayana and Mahabharata have been adapted into various languages and styles. From the early days of Indian cinema, both epics have been adapted into films, and more recently, television series. These adaptations often bring new interpretations and perspectives to the classic stories. Additionally, the epics have been adapted into animation and graphic novels for children, making them accessible to a wide audience.

In recent years, the epics have been adapted into a number of Bollywood movies, which have gained popularity not only in India but also in other parts of the world. For example, in 2020 the movie "Tanhaji: The Unsung Warrior" which is based on the life of a Maratha warrior who fought in the battle of Sinhagad during the 17th century. The movie is inspired by the Mahabharata, and it was a critical and commercial success.

In other countries, the Ramayana and Mahabharata have been adapted into movies and TV shows in various languages such as in Indonesia, the Ramayana is known as the Ramakien, and has been adapted into films, television series, and wayang (shadow puppet) performances.

The Ramayana and Mahabharata are two of the most important and enduring texts in Indian culture, and their influence can be seen in many forms of modern literature and film. They have been retold, reinterpreted, and adapted into various forms such as novels, poetry, plays, films, television series, animation and graphic novels, making them accessible to a wide audience. The epics have also been adapted into Bollywood movies, which have gained popularity not only in India but also in other parts of the world and adapted into other languages and cultures, such as in Indonesia.

ᴩᴩᴩ

"You are the embodiment of your deepest, most driving desires. Your will is determined by your desires, and your actions are determined by your will. Ultimately, your destiny is determined by your deeds." - Brihadaranyaka Upanishad

TWELVE

THE RAMAYANA AND MAHABHARATA IN CONTEMPORARY INDIAN SOCIETY

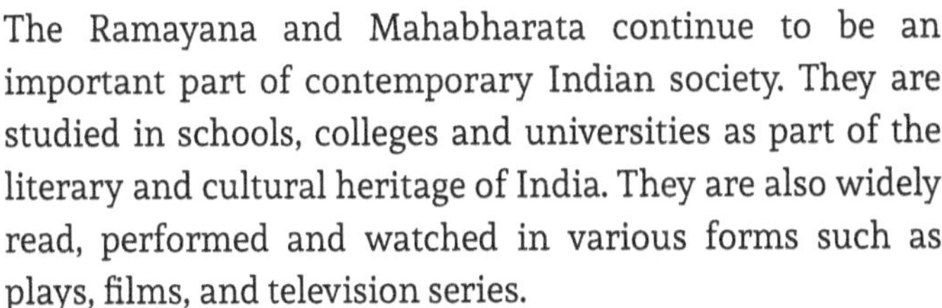

The Ramayana and Mahabharata continue to be an important part of contemporary Indian society. They are studied in schools, colleges and universities as part of the literary and cultural heritage of India. They are also widely read, performed and watched in various forms such as plays, films, and television series.

The stories and characters of these epics are deeply ingrained in the collective consciousness of the Indian people, and they continue to shape the cultural and moral values of contemporary Indian society. The characters of Rama and Krishna, in particular, are widely revered and considered as role models for morality and ethics. They are often invoked in religious rituals and ceremonies, and their stories are used to teach important lessons about duty, loyalty, and the importance of following one's dharma (moral and ethical code).

The stories of the Ramayana and Mahabharata also provide a cultural context for many of the customs and traditions of India. For example, the festival of Diwali, which celebrates the return of Rama to Ayodhya after his victory over Ravana, is widely celebrated in India and is considered one of the most important festivals of the year.

Additionally, the themes of the epics have been adapted to address contemporary issues and concerns. For example, the story of the Ramayana has been used to promote gender equality, and the story of the Mahabharata has been used to promote the idea of non-violence.

The Ramayana and Mahabharata continue to be an important part of contemporary Indian society, shaping the cultural and moral values of the people. They are widely read, performed and watched in various forms such as plays, films, and television series. The stories and characters of these epics are deeply ingrained in the collective consciousness of the Indian people and provide a cultural context for many of the customs and traditions of India. The themes of the epics have also been adapted to address contemporary issues and concerns.

ᐅᐅᐅ

To revere our mothers, fathers, teachers, and guests as divine beings is a sacred act. We can honor them by treating them with the utmost respect and admiration, as if they were gods. Doing so is a way of expressing our gratitude for all that they have done for us. It is also a way of showing our appreciation for the wisdom and guidance they have provided us. By treating them with reverence, we can demonstrate our commitment to upholding the highest standards of morality and integrity. - The Taittiriya Upanishad

THIRTEEN

ALTERNATIVE INTERPRETATIONS OF THE RAMAYANA AND MAHABHARATA

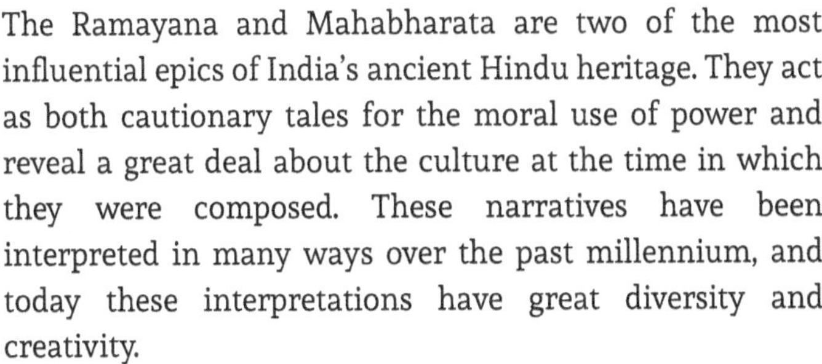

The Ramayana and Mahabharata are two of the most influential epics of India's ancient Hindu heritage. They act as both cautionary tales for the moral use of power and reveal a great deal about the culture at the time in which they were composed. These narratives have been interpreted in many ways over the past millennium, and today these interpretations have great diversity and creativity.

One interpretation of these epics is the study of Dharma and its relation to human existence. Dharma is the concept of maintaining balance in the universe. It is believed that by living a life in harmony with cosmic laws and guided by principles that are good and virtuous, one can break the cycle of birth and rebirth and obtain spiritual enlightenment. The epics emphasize that this challenge is greater when social and political values are at stake, as is the case in both these epics.

The Ramayana and Mahabharata also have mythological roots to them as well that can be interpreted. Both narratives feature many divine beings and powerful characters who transcend traditional morality and possess qualities that are labeled as divine. Thus, mythological interpretations focus on the idea that following divine principles will lead to the establishment of justice and strife-free society.

The epics can also be interpreted as reflections of the politics of the day. Many believe that the struggles between the main characters in the Ramayana and Mahabharata were used as metaphors for the religious clashes and political tensions of the times. Political interpretations of the epics view them as examples of ancient strategies for resolving conflicts.

Finally, the Ramayana and Mahabharata can also be interpreted as allegorical tales. In this way they symbolize the psychological and spiritual development of the individual. It is believed that the choices the characters make mirror the struggles of the individual's mind and heart and their search for the true meaning of life.

Ultimately, it is clear that there are a multitude of ways

to interpret the Ramayana and Mahabharata, and all interpretations offer a great deal of insight into the culture and history of India. Although interpretations often differ, the core messages of morality, sacredness of life and responsibility to society are universal and timeless.

ᗰᗰᗰ

The body is said to be a temple, and the soul is truly Shiva. Discard the faded flower offerings of ignorance and instead worship with the thought: "I am He". – Maitreya Upanishad

FOURTEEN

THE RAMAYANA AND MAHABHARATA IN SOUTHEAST ASIAN CULTURE

The Ramayana and Mahabharata have had a significant impact on Southeast Asian culture and continue to be an important part of the cultural heritage of many countries in the region.

In Indonesia, the Ramayana is known as the Ramakien, and has been adapted into various forms such as wayang (shadow puppet) performances, dance dramas, and films. The story of the Ramayana is deeply ingrained in the cultural consciousness of the Indonesian people and is widely performed and watched.

In Thailand, the Ramakien is also an important part of the cultural heritage and is regularly performed in the form of dance dramas, puppet shows, and other forms of traditional theater. The Ramakien is also taught in schools as part of the national curriculum and is considered a fundamental part of Thai culture.

In Cambodia, the Ramayana is known as the Reamker, and has been an important part of Cambodian culture for centuries. The Reamker is regularly performed in the form of dance dramas and shadow puppetry and it is also taught in schools as part of the national curriculum.

In other Southeast Asian countries such as Laos, Vietnam, and Malaysia, the Ramayana and Mahabharata have also been adapted and retold in various forms, such as plays, films, and television series, and continue to be an important part of the cultural heritage.

The Ramayana and Mahabharata have had a significant impact on Southeast Asian culture, and continue to be an important part of the cultural heritage of many countries in the region. In Indonesia, Thailand, and Cambodia, the Ramayana is known as Ramakien and is widely performed and watched, taught in schools as part of the national curriculum and considered a fundamental part of the culture. In other Southeast Asian countries, the epics have also been adapted and retold in various forms, and continue to be an important part of the cultural heritage.

ᎣᎣᎣ

Those who recognize the unity of all life, seeing themselves in all creatures and all creatures in themselves, know no fear or grief. How can the multiplicity of life deceive the one who perceives its oneness? – Isha Upanishad

FIFTEEN

THE RAMAYANA AND MAHABHARATA AND THE ENVIRONMENT

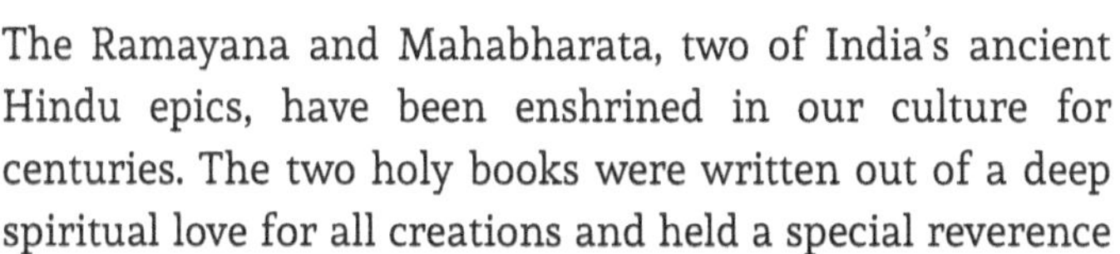

The Ramayana and Mahabharata, two of India's ancient Hindu epics, have been enshrined in our culture for centuries. The two holy books were written out of a deep spiritual love for all creations and held a special reverence for the environment.

In these ancient works, nature was seen as a place of renewal, a place to return to our true selves, and as a provider of sustenance. Rama, the hero of the Ramayana, taught us to be gentle and caring with our surroundings, to protect and be kind to animals, and to honor the great balance of nature. He lived out his message through example, embodying respect for all living creatures.

In the Mahabharata, the Pandavas, the five brothers, served their elders and showed respect for their environment. They explored the beauty of the land and respected the trees, birds, and animals. Yudhishthira, the eldest Pandava, demonstrated great wisdom and taught us that humankind should develop with nature, not against it. He represented the polarity between the human and the natural world and showed us that the strength of nature lies in the balance of the two.

Other characters in the Mahabharata demonstrate how to nurture nature, such as Krishna and his cowgirls, who taught us how to nurture the environment and recognize our place in it. They showed us that sustainable practices can lead to greater harmony with nature.

The epics of the Ramayana and Mahabharata have influenced our values and beliefs for centuries and offer valuable insights on how to live harmoniously with the environment. They teach us that living with nature does not mean exploiting it, but rather coexisting with it and bringing about great rewards for all creatures. If we take this lesson to heart and emulate these great stories, our environment can once again become a place of vibrancy and life.

ppp

Other Books Of The Author

1. The Moments When I Met God
2. Kashiyile Theertha Pathangal
3. GURU GYAN VANI
4. Abhiprerak Gita
5. ASSI SE JAIN GHAT TAK
6. Hopelessness of Arjuna
7. The Soul and It's True Nature
8. Sense of Action (Karma)
9. Action through Wisdom
10. Action through Wisdom
11. THEORY AND PRACTICAL OF EVERY ACTION
12. LOGICAL UNDERSTANDING OF THE SUPREME
13. THE IMPERISHABLE SUPREME
14. Yatra Nishadraj se Hanuman Ghat Tak
15. Yatra Karnatak Ghat se Raja Ghat Tak
16. Yatra Pandey Ghat se Prayagraj Ghat Tak
17. Yatra Ranjendra Prasad Ghat se Dattatreya Ghat Tak
18. YaatraSindhiya Ghat se Gwaliar Ghat Tak
19. Yatra Mangala Gauri Ghat se Hanuman Gadhi Ghat Tak
20. Yatra Gaay Ghat Se Nishad Ghat Tak
21. MAA GANGA, GHATEN EVM UTSAV
22. Ganga Arti Dev Deepavali evam Any Utsav
23. Potentials of Digitalized India
24. VEDIC CONSCIOUSNESS
25. A Brief Introduction to Vedic Science
26. Kashi ke Barah Jyotirling
27. IMPACT OF MOTIVATION
28. Let's have a Milky Way Journey
29. Color Therapy in a Nutshell

30. Rigveda in a Nutshell
31. Yajurveda in a Nutshell
32. Samveda in a Nutshell
33. Atharva Veda in a Nutshell
34. Ayushman Bhava - Ayurveda
35. Srimad Bhagavad Gita and Upanishad Connection
36. Srimad Bhagavad Gita - an attempt to summarize each chapter.
37. Facts and Impact of Nakshatra
38. Astro Gems - NAVARATNA
39. Ekadashi - A Concise Overview
40. A Concise View of Hanuman Chalisa
41. Inspirational Gita
42. Nakshatraranyam
43. Summary of 18 Mahapuranas
44. Synopsis of 18 Upa Puranas
45. Rigvediya Upanishads
46. Shukla Yajurvediya Upanishads
47. Krishna Yajurvediya Upanishads
48. Samavediya Upanishads
49. Atharvavediya Upanishads
50. The Seven Great Sages
51. From Rocket Scientist to President Dr. APJ Abdul Kalam
52. The Visionary's Voice - Quotes of Dr. APJ Abdul Kalam
53. The Wisdom of Swami Vivekananda: Insights and Inspiration from a Legendary Spiritual Teacher
54. Ayurvedic Remedies from the Garden
55. Sages and Seers
56. Rising Strong – Motivational Stories of Women
57. Beyond Flames -Mystery stories of Funeral Ghat Manikarnika
58. The Origins of Tulsi: A Look at the Mythological Roots of the Plant"

59. The Holistic Cow: A Look at the Physical, Spiritual, and Cultural Importance of Cows in India
60. Arts of Healing
61. Exploring the Divine
62. Understanding Five Elements
63. The Etymology of Ram
64. Symbols of India
65. Voice of Change (About Speeches of Great Men)
66. She Speaks (About Speeches of Great Women)
67. Patriotism on Celluloid – Brief About Patriotic Films
68. The Music of Motivation: A Brief Guide to Inspirational Film Songs
69. Unlocking the Secrets of the Dashopanishads
70. A Cultural Mosaic
71. Ancient Traditions, Modern Minds
72. Ecos of Ancient Wisdom
73. Beneath the Surface
74. From Temples to Ashrams
75. Sages of the Subcontinent
76. The Art of Healling (Ayurveda, Yoga & Naturopathy)
77. Indian Kitchen
78. The Festivals of India

❧❧❧

Contact

DR. JAGADEESH PILLAI

PhD in Vedic Science

Four Times Guinness World Record Holder

Winner of Mahatma Gandhi Vishwa Shanti Puraskar and
Global Peace Ambassador

Gemology, Astro & Vastu Consultant - Spiritual Counselor

Consultant for designing World Record Ideas

Efficient Tarot Card Reader

9839093003

myrichindia@gmail.com

drjagadeeshpillai@facebook

drjagadeeshpillai@instagram

jagadeeshpillai@youtube

www. JAGADEESHPILLAI.com

▷▷▷

|| LOKAHA SAMASTHAHA SUKHINO BHAVANTU ||

• 73 •

www.ingramcontent.com/pod-product-compliance
Lightning Source LLC
Chambersburg PA
CBHW022228160726
47991CB00017B/2700